maya

The University of Massachusetts Press   Amherst, 1979

ELEANOR WILNER

The author would like to express her gratitude to the
National Endowment for the Arts, for the Creative
Writing Grant which enabled her to complete this
manuscript.

"Epitaph," "Unstrung," "For a Poet of Nature," and
"Water Lace and White Eyes" first appeared in *Poetry*
126, no. 3 (June 1975); "Knowing the Enemy" and
"A Private Space" first appeared in *The Minnesota
Review,* NS 6 (Spring 1976), reprinted in *The Bore-
stone Mountain Poetry Awards 1977: Best Poems of
1976;* "Journey from the East" first appeared in
Mother Jones 2, no. 1 (January 1977); "Iphigenia,
Setting the Record Straight" and "Natural History"
first appeared in *Calyx* 3, no. 3 (February 1979);
"Landing," "Bailing Out—A Poem for the 1970s,"
"Closing Ceremonies for the Bicentennial," "Posthu-
mous Poem," and "A Comment on the Relevance of
Modern Science to the Everyday Lives of the Larger
Animals" first appeared in *Calyx* 4, no. 1 (June 1979);
"Laurels" first appeared in *The New Republic* (May
1979); "Beyond the Second Landing" first appeared
in *The New Republic* (July 1979).

To my grandmother, Etta Rand
this book is dedicated with love

Contents

iv. Attrition

v. Illuminated Manuscripts

i. Effigies

It was a pure white cloud that hung there
in the blue, or a jellyfish on a waveless
sea, suspended high above us; we were
the creatures in the weeds below.
It seemed so effortless in its suspense,
perfectly out of time and out of place
like the ghost of moon in the sky
of a brilliant afternoon.
After a while it seemed to grow, and we
inferred that it was moving, drifting down—
though it seemed weightless, motionless,
one of those things that defy
the usual forces—gravity, and wind
and the almost imperceptible
pressure of the years. But it was coming
down.
              The blur of its outline slowly cleared:
it was scalloped at the lower edge, like a shell
or a child's drawing of a flower, detached
and floating, beauty simplified. That's when
we saw it had a man attached, suspended
from the center of the flower, a kind of human
stamen or a stem. We thought it was
a god, or heavenly seed, sent
to germinate the earth
with a gentler, nobler breed. It might be
someone with sunlit eyes and a mind of dawn.
We thought of falling to our knees.

So you can guess
the way we might have felt
when it landed in our field
with the hard thud of solid flesh
and the terrible flutter of the collapsing
lung of silk. He smelled of old sweat, his
uniform was torn, and he was tangled
in the ropes, hopelessly harnessed
to the white mirage that brought him down.
He had a wound in his chest, a red
flower that took its color from his heart.

3

We buried him that very day, just as he came
to us, in a uniform of soft brown
with an eagle embroidered on the sleeve,
its body made of careful gray stitches,
its eye a knot of gold. The motto
underneath had almost worn away. For days,
watching from our caves, we saw
the huge white shape of silk shifting
in the weeds, like a pale moon
when the wind filled it, stranded,
searching in the aimless way
of unmoored things
for whatever human ballast gave
direction to their endless drift.

4

Though only a girl,
the first born of the Pharoah,
I was the first to die.

Young then,
we were bored already,
rouged pink as oleanders
on the palace grounds, petted
by the eunuchs, overfed
from gem-encrusted bowls, barren
with wealth, until the hours of the afternoon
seemed to outlast even
my grandmother's mummy, a perfect
little dried apricot
in a golden skin. We would paint
to pass the time, with delicate
brushes dipped in char
on clay, or on our own blank lids.
So it was that day we found him
wailing in the reeds, he seemed
a miracle to us, plucked
from the lotus by the ibis' beak,
the squalling seed of the sacred
Nile. He was permitted
as a toy; while I pretended play
I honed him like a sword.
For him, I was as polished and as perfect
as a pebble in a stutterer's mouth.
While the slaves' fans beat
incessantly as insect wings,
I taught him how to hate
this painted Pharoah's tomb
this palace built of brick
and dung, and gilded like a poet's
tongue; these painted eyes.

"Or set upon a golden bough to sing
   To lords and ladies of Byzantium
   Of what is past, or passing, or to come."

It was a jewelled tapestry:
cut rubies hung for fruit
from the trees; lilies sewn into the ground;
the eyes of the unicorn were pearl
his horn a twist of ivory
his mane a fringe of silk.
The lady was all brocade and lace
her feet impossibly small in scarlet stuff
a satin band around her waist
divided her neatly in two.
The moon was a cluster of seed pearls—
a silver pomegranate with the skin half gone.
The toy dog's tongue was a shameless red
as if the blood had run into the thread
dyed beyond the possibility of death.
And the eye of the little bird
glittered more impatiently than gems;
it tried its beak on its own gold coat
that tied it to the branch—tore it
stitch by stitch, to shreds
and danced in its naked bones, fragile
as the structure of a dream, or the anatomy
of lace; its call, a drop of rain
sliding down a single silver wire.
It flew into the night— a stroke
or two of chalk wiped off a slate.

The clock strikes; the bony spire of the church
is a black splinter
in the dead white thumb of moon.
The mouse comes out to forage for its young
looks up and sees, with widening eyes
the bat, who cannot see
as it sinks its teeth in trembling fur
a face so like its own.

Opinions, we only seemed to hold, to hoe
the ordinary fields—in fact, we were, like him,
cunning by nature, natural only
by adoption; finding, in the vast irrelevance
of green, a hiding place with a good name.
We, who couldn't really plow a field, or
bring the rich mud tumble of the earth
to bear, took refuge in the dappled light,
in mist, in trellises
where the tendrils of the vine
tangled the light as it broke
through reluctance into shade. Let us admit
this green was a filter and a frame
and not the living shelter that it seemed.
Through it, we held the light at bay,
though it spotted our skin until we were afraid
of the camouflage we had become.
Like children seeking power over loss, we had
begun a game of hide and seek, and
by the odd coincidence of need
or scarcity of places left
to hide, had stumbled into the same arbor.

If we could have said, then, why we had come
and having touched, dispelled the play
of light that made our skin seem lace
instead of flesh, perhaps—
but we did not. By then, we had become
the figures in a shadow play, and were so wholly
other to ourselves, that nothing much was said.
The sun caught the trellis ladder in the light,
showing where the paint was flaking off the wood,
how many of the vines were dead,
how intricate the weaving was, how admirable
the whole design.

7

"The hard snow held me, save where now and then
   One foot went through."
                    Robert Frost, "The Wood-Pile"

An owl, newly blinded by the moon, lit
on a branch above his head. The eyes
of the owl opened slowly, like two
sliding doors, and the man passed through.
Inside it was all gray, the sky
a solid silver dome, like the inside
of Athena's helmet. Clouds rose
from fissures in the ground like frozen
breath. The rivers lay unmoving as
poured lead. He could feel his hair and nails
growing. A woman stood at the juncture
of two hills, complicated by a stand
of crystal ferns, snow
falling from her eyes. As he approached
he felt the torn lace wings of moths
brush back and forth across his face.
She moved away and where she walked
the ground turned glass, the surface
chimed. He tried again to follow.
But the glass shattered under
his feet, and he broke through, falling
among the bits of broken ice, but slower
as a feather falls through air. She
was far above him now, the edge
of her skirt fluttering
in the jagged opening
cut in the shape of a man.

His outline faded as he fell away from it,
grew smaller till it might have been
a distant bird, arrested in mid-flight.

and the mist rising
as the temperature climbs toward dawn.
It is nearly morning, nearly spring—
whispers between darkness and the light:
white clouds out of the mouth, sun
at the back of the mind.
The white mailed fist loosens its grip
on the blue river; the birds circle
following the compass of their wings
to make a hollow nest of air.
At the far edge a sled appears,
the driver wrapped in furs, relics
of the hunt, his face hard
under the helmet of frost, a sculpture
for the wind to
whittle to a fine edge. The geese settle
on the inland floes, their beaks pry
into the filigree of water lace;
the bear's paw
dips and flashes in the rising sun.

Twin dogs halt the half-disordered
team, the driver frozen at the reins
a Cid in the armor of the frost
moored in the drifts, his eyes white—
burned out by the light that blazed
for days across the ice. One by one
the dogs lie down, their ears laid back
in the signal of alarm, their tongues
loll red among the white crags
of their teeth. They whine, harnessed
to the sledge of bones lashed tight in place
with leather thongs, runners deep
in the drifted snow. The sun leaks
red between the hills, the dogs
cower at the rising scent
of what their driver, thawing, has become.
Suddenly, they pull
toward the four corners
of the frozen earth, like some six-headed
sinewy beast, or snowflake changed
to flesh and fur, intent—

in the growing light and unrelenting reins—
on tearing itself apart:
dead center
in the Northern dawn.

10

ii. Departures

The yogi sits on the burning rock, a drying skin
that has shed its snake. His beggar's bowl
is empty as a skull; the sky *nir-vana*, without the wind.
His eyes are waterless and shed
tears neither for the dead nor those
who drag themselves through doors
to start the daily round again.
He is vacant as the space between two stars.
He lets the lion claws of sun
rake him unopposed. Chameleons, mistaking him
for stone, stretch out on him to take the sun
and lose their color to his own.
And still he sits, transparent soul,
a blister on the earth's brown back.

The woman, says the holy man, can never
escape from *maya*; it grows in her like maggots
in tainted meat, and drives her from his holy ground.

She runs, down the grassy path by which she came;
her passage stirs the grass to dancing. *Maya
maya* . . . as she goes down, the growth thickens
the green and tangled forest takes her in.
Her skin is like the fawn's—indelibly marked
with sun and shade: in safety, ornament;
in danger, camouflage. When she sinks down
among the twisted vines and sleeps,
the darkness gathers at the center
of her eyes, the pupil of the moon
under a covering of cloud. *Maya, maya* . . .
everything is close to everything, the stars
hang among the woven branches of the trees,
the moon is a lantern overgrown with leaves.
The first light rises from the steaming
earth; a heron lifts his head, his long legs
reeds that awkwardly step
out of their roots and walk, as the sun
opens his great yellow eye and lowers
his gaze, veiled by the lashes of the ferns.
A fish with golden scales leaps
through the shadow of the woman
as she bends to drink.

13

Maya, maya . . . this veil is my skin
that hides me from him
who sees nothing.

14

The sun strikes the whale's back;
he dives, until the sun is overcast
with tons of green. He knows himself
full-grown; the burden that he carried
in his belly like a stone, is gone;
he has given his Jonah back to God.

For years he carried him, under
the furrowed trenches of his brow
and felt him walk by day the caves
under the great hill of his back—
this memory, this earth-bound being
he had been. Since he was small

this manthing had been tangled in
the mangroves of his mind; burning
like swampfire, or the hated sun,
searing him who needed filtered light,
for whom the mist was heaven.
Such preferences are fate.

When, with a great heave, he disgorged
this image that distended him,
he found it strange
how puny his antagonist had grown—
a twin-tailed tadpole
flashing off in foam.

His silver geyser rises in the air;
the bad dreams disappear
like islands off his starboard flank.
He moves, huge, through his own mist,
oiled silver by the moon, arrowed
as St. Sebastian, bristling harpoons.

15

with neither bones nor skin
swims in the green haze of a golden sea
shot through with sun that tangles
in the weeds, like the woven filaments
of tapestry. Playful, he skims the tops of waves
like a skipped stone; plumbs the green depths
not as a stone falls, but
as a swimmer dives for his own delight.
On a still night, when you think you see the moon
stare back at you from the surface of a pond,
it may not be a mere reflected light,
twice-removed from the sun—but the round fish
regarding you, as a man may stare intently
at a mirror, trying, through the too familiar face
to catch a glimpse of someone half-perceived.
It is no trick of mirrors, no infinite regress
of self-regarding mind, but the round fish
regarding you, recovering his own.

I watched a man one night, by a stream,
transfixed by the round fish, until he broke
the water with his hand, wanting to scoop
it out, like some demented bear, all his cunning
in his paw. When he drew back his arm,
his hand was silver to the wrist.

That night I dreamed of swimming, far out
at sea, beyond the line of reefs, easy
as you swim in dreams. And the round fish
with neither bones nor skin
swam near, the sky blazed blue, the fish
was rainbow-hued, right before he disappeared.
Surprised, I saw a jut of land I hadn't seen before
and climbed ashore, following the tracks
the fish had left, which fit so strangely
with my own. The trail now is not so fresh,
harder to follow in the undergrowth; still
it was something to have been started on at all;
it hardly matters that, where the sea turns
into land and the growth thickens—you no longer know
the trail you take
from the one that you are making as you go.

The wise men had grown heavy
in their flesh, and in their
dreams: that dull report of what
they'd mastered. And their camels
found it harder than before
to rise from their knees.

The child they sought
was no one in particular. Just the sun
regaining its warmth, a flourish of green
in the midst of winter, a simple solstice
of the soul.
       When they had left their burdens—
the jewels and fine perfumes, the gold—
they dropped their robes of purple,
stepped out of them
into the night, leaving no one
the wiser.
       They walked unnoticed
out of myth, their beards flowing in the hot
desert wind, winter broken
in their minds, their steps lighter
than anyone imagines.

He never knew, the child,
high on incense in his mother's arms,
that his recurring dream
of a time when kings would vanish from the earth
was just the memory of that night,
the gift
of that unheralded departure.

17

You can watch the sky from here, a fabled tower
by the sea, while the gulls wheel,
see with a double eye—here, a silver flash
of fish, there, the gray unmoving
cliffs. You could stay for years—Tasso's
black queen of Ethiopia
locked in a turret by a jealous mate
staring at the murals of an alien myth
bearing a snow-white child to suit
a Christian sense of miracle.
                                        Or,
some night, when the jailers
are drugged with wine or
nodding on hashish—you could go
in a slow circle down the stairs
with a single lamp to throw your shadow
in your path; so darkened by your own descent
gain the beach, wade out until your skirts
are ruffled with the tide, the tower
a black finger held against the night—
an admonition to be still. You could make a sail
of your skirt, hoist it on a stolen craft, outrun
the storyteller's art and cheat the knights
clattering in their ill-joined iron suits
of a certain rescue. Then the singer in the court
who weaves more verses than the oak has leaves
would find his fingers fallen from the strings
the next line hanging in the air
      a vine the wind has torn from the wall.

   Listen, the foam is whispering;
far out at sea, the stormy petrel
like some charred spirit from a burnt-out hell
her wings spread wide, tries the freshening wind.

18

Henry Adams' Wife in Washington, D.C.

It was her idea to go there.
She wanted to see the grave
of Henry Adams' wife. The statue
there had some repute; her interest
had been sharpened by a tourist's pen:
the right sort, the class of visitor
who follows his taste through boxwood
to find those impeccable moments
the unsuspecting never miss. She had read
it years before, and written it down.
Now I took her there, the sort of guide
who follows the whims of her elders.

She was seated in the half-shade, a
shade tree at her side, its leaves
dark green as old plush, but waxed
and gleaming as the furniture
in Georgetown shops. She was perfectly
composed. She had a mantle, of the antique
kind, drawn over her head; it cast
a gentle darkness over her impassive
finely molded cheek. I think she was called
Peace. Her folded hands
were elegant marble gloves, beyond the need
of knitting needles or embroidery
to keep them calm. Even the birds
had not intruded on her privacy.
In fact, she was so sheltered in the green,
we would never have found her
if we hadn't asked the guard.

I don't know Henry Adams' wife
from Adam's. Nor who that sculptor was
who could embody such sufficiency
while on commission. And couldn't,
even if I tried, become
the kind of guide to find again
such fine repose in stone.

The woman whose idea it was
had drawn her tweed coat tighter to her chest
and sighed. "She is perfect," she said.
"She doesn't need anybody."
And spoke, with that, her own, flat epitaph.

The towers waited, shimmering just
beyond the edge of vision.
It was only a question
of wind, of the command of trade routes,
a narrow isthmus between two seas, possession
of the gold that men called Helen.
The oldest of adulteries: trade
and art. We were to wait
for the outcome, to see
if we would be the vassals of a king,
or the slaves of slaves.

They never found my grave, who was supposed
to fill their sails, like the skirts of women,
with her charms. Helen, as the second version
goes, had stayed at home; only the echo
of the rustle of her robes
went with Paris to the high-walled town. I
stayed with her to the end, this aunt of mine,
and friend, whose illness drove her husband out the door,
dull-witted Menelaus. When she died
the swans deserted the palace pool
and the torches flared dark
and fitfully. I did not stay for their return,
like that foolish Electra.

I hid in the shrine of Athena—
hearing her, nights, pace overhead
with an iron step, like the sound
of the bronze age ending. The old blind
singer in the forecourt
must have heard her too, but
unlike me, he had to make his living
from his song. She was often sleepless,
as gods will be, and the nights went slow
under her heel's heavy tread.
When she went to stay the arm of
great Achilles, to save my father
for my mother's knife—
I slipped away.

I have just been living, quiet, in this little village
on goats I keep for cheese and sell for wine, unknown—
the praise of me on every lip, the me
my father made up in his mind
and sacrificed for wind.

21

—for Stephanie Sugioka

This is the space where
the question of beauty enters,
in soft slippers, decorous, even a little
obsequious, muted
as if by choice. She kneels with
her pot of steaming tea; as she pours,
the long black screen of hair
falls across her face.
She handles her limbs
as if they were porcelain. She is almost
perfect, except for the space,
the shadowed gap,
in her huge kimono sleeves.
A hint of silver flashes
in that dark, a sliver of moon
on a night in September, the silk
chrysanthemums nodding
like conspirators along the hem
of sky.

(The icon painters of a thousand years ago
always left a little space unfinished
somewhere in the work. It was the place,
they said, inviting to the soul—
where the singular could enter the design,
the ultimate intensity of a slight
intrusion.)

One silver stroke: her eyes opened wide
as ivory fans at the flick of a wrist.
The moon slips through the silk
wrappings of the clouds. Later
she would pass through the rooms,
through the lines of mourners, like light
through the elegant
black lacquered slats of blinds, slender
and bright
beyond suspicion.

22

iii. Histories

We thought our arms
were like the lowest branches
on the trees, that, reaching out,
prevent the top from growing, grazing stars.
For years, for centuries, we pruned away
the parts permitting touch. First the twigs,
compassionate with buds, then
the whole branch, scarring
the trunk where the sap oozed out, hardened
into amber. And the tops grew
high as spires, so tall you couldn't
hear the birds in them, and when
wind stirred the leaves, the rustle
was so distant—we thought it
angels. We were armless then
as torsos of ancient marble dug
from sunken ships and set
on pedestals, eloquent with loss, speaking
of an old perfection—some balance struck
between the chisel and the heart.

But lately, there is a tingling where
our fingers used to be: the bright
excruciating pain of blood
returning to the numb.

We are still trying out our stiff new
limbs, touching things the way
the blind read   the language
made   by puncturing
the page,   letting in
the light.

25

"How do you like to go up in a swing,
  Up in the air so blue?
Oh, I do think it the pleasantest thing
  Ever a child can do!"

From a place like ours, safe
on the garden swing—who could have dreamed
our history: the rocks of undiluted red,
raw color, burning sands, the terrible
hot mouths of volcanoes. Or beasts of leather
and of bone, cruising
the orange skies, blood running black as oil
in the fissures where the rock was torn.
Or known the continent of ice
with its cutting edge, moving ponderously
across the face of a resisting earth
until it pressed small lives into the stone
like a botanist his flowers in a book.

These things were beyond us, children
reading Stevenson, the poet proved
for the likes of us—lives measured
by the rope's arc on the swing.
We were permitted views from that high seat—
seen through the eyes of little English
children: soft gardens, tipped in
gladiolas, gently rouged with the pink
of roses; beyond them, distant hills, blue
fading to . . . fade was too weak a word
for what was happening out there: the world
grew blurred and shrank and disappeared.
By then, the rope had reached the limit
of its arc, and pulled us back, giddy
with distance but coming down.
It was like the careful meters of
the poet—a sickly child, playing soldiers
on the counterpane. Between
the contours of those ironed hills
and the glacial smoothness of the sheet
below, asleep or reading, we first found
that other place, the one that was hidden till
you lifted the sheet of red
cellophane off the page—and towers loomed, imps

appeared. And something beyond the garden swing:
something you must have seen
but never mentioned. So that we came
to it, without a guide, wide-eyed,
trying to build the red bricks
of the garden wall back over it,
but failing, even then,
beginning to fail.

27

She wore the skins of animals,
laced up boots, a bright babushka
on her head. Every well was full
of witches, and the bodies of men
cried murder, or sweet love.
Icicles hung from the barns
and when she sought her image
in the pond, the ice was blank.
The geese wore a necklace of
frost, and everything shimmered
in the timid sun. The shadows
of the branches were scribbled
on the snow. When she saw
old women, bent back, humping
down the road, she'd run for cover
in the glittering wood, where little birds
chattered like teeth.

    It was in such a season, near
a place with a Russian name, the village
gathered in a circle on the snow,
began the dance, slow at first,
boots pounding the frozen earth,
ermine clouds trimming the air.
    They had put her in the center
with the bear, the iron chain around his neck
biting deep in the brown fur.
The dance quickened as the sun
caught the tops of firs, the yellow burning
through the green. Looking up, she seemed to see
from the weedy bottom of a well.
And the world spun
in the sun and in the centrifuge
of clan—it was then
the bear broke loose. He rose
until he blotted out the light—
deep in his throat a sound
like the ice breaking up
in the bay outside St. Petersburg,
the thunder of the spring.

They hunted the bear for days,
but could make nothing of his broken
tracks that bent and doubled back,
and disappeared.
                The girl was a long time
healing. The slash from one wild claw
had slit her face from hair to chin.
When it closed, it seamed her face
with a rope of red; by fall
it was a slender line, indecipherable,
like the road where it vanishes in wood
and you have to turn around
to get back to the village
before dark.

29

There are beads on the ice, sweat
on the forehead of the caveman
thawing in the block, fear
on his half-formed brow. As a boat
slides free of winter, its prow
fronting the green waves with a groan of boards,
the caveman in the ice begins to stir.
He puts his hand out to the ice,
he puts his hand through into air, and
stares because it isn't there, because he has
to draw a breath, to step
into the place that's gone, because
he must depend on *that.*

If only he could stop
the steaming of his flesh, the labor
of his lungs, the sting of salt
on all his limbs, that weight
he never felt till now.
He takes another breath, breathes
out: a little cloud forms
from his mouth. The clouds are coming faster
now; uttering white and soundless shapes,
he follows them across the snow.

He doesn't know his track
is in the ground, the half-moons
of his heels, the ten round grooves of toe—
he only knows the condensation of his heat
in air, imagines there a trail
of perfect forms; he doesn't see behind him as
they vanish into air. Only his spoor
remains to steam, to bring
the team that's after him: the one
whose guns restore him
to the ice, the solid world he wanted
to get back to, the one
that he was always tracking.

When had the snails stopped
their slow tracing of the sand, begun
to pile up outside the palace door,
nothing now but hollow ciphers,
numbered stones, the ruined squares
of courts, the delicate concentric circles
of the shells, the hot and dusty
summer air, the trees
thick and throbbing with cicadas, the lizard's
heat a pale permutation of the sun.

The site was low, set so the nearby hills
cut off the view of sea.
From time to time a leaf dipped
under the weight of a bee, or a green-eyed
bottlefly buzzed, an old saw
rasping on wood. Two villagers, both nondescript,
were paid to guard the place and sat unmoved
as dead grass on a day without wind.

Too much sun and the rain balks; time
writes with chalk on the land; the ground bakes
harder than unleavened bread; the fruit stays
small on the branch, curled up
like the fists of stillborn sons.
The mules are no more stubborn than the hills
whose cracked and stony backs ignore
the sticks that try to beat them into life.

A crescent moon of bone, the horns
still guard the outer wall, cradle the empty air:
a distance so intense, you can hear the blue.
Here, no one speaks, as if the human voice
were brittle and would break
like potsherds in the dust, the code
that was broken, after all.

With any luck, you might find one piece
still intact, a perfect spiral baked in clay,
unwind the skein again—the snails stir,
a pink face and a pair of horns start
from every shell; hear, far below, the bull
pawing the earth again
with one stone hoof.

Care, carefully chosen, even
more carefully marked—the dazed white stone,
glass of compression. One wrong move, one
slip of the chisel—pressure
improperly brought to bear,
a trembling hand, any
of a hundred miscalculations, and
splinters: the shattered chance
in a million—the perfect split.

Perhaps I am mistaken. Perhaps
the glitter is only dust
on the workbench, a trifle struck
by sun. Is it ordinary dust
that dazzles us or
some important failure: the intractable
reduced in that encounter
with intention, dancing now
in a beam of light falling through the window—
failed in all but its resistance
to design?

32

Enormous, the upper brain
rests uneasy on its stalk, unsteady
as the infant head on its delicate stem.
The little ape of love
and appetite fastens its long, slim
fingers to the stem and climbs
toward the huge gray mass of clouds
where giants laugh, holding their
immense sides, their castles of stone
swaying on thin green stalks.

Why does the giant have
the small black glittering eyes
of the rhesus monkey?
And why does the little monkey-man
going hand over hand
up the earth-driven vine to the sky
have eyes as wide as mountain lakes, soft
as the down that grows under the tongues,
under the wings, of angels?

What was it started us
up the long green ladder to the stars?
Who took the blue dome of our days
and darkened it, punched it full of brilliant
holes, each one dangling a long gold filament
of light we try to climb as if to storm
the walls of heaven?

Who waits up there
at the top of our heads, like some evolutionary
dare, taunting us, turning away
from our decay, wanting our blood, pretending
not to share our hungers? Has visions like
the crystal clouds we breathe
when animal heat encounters winter air?

33

Begin again. It is morning and a time
for simple talk. Here, a little monkey-man
holds another against his furred and fragrant
breast, and the strange trees, with their
overbearing tops, heavy as the willow
in summer, in snow, bend down
and brush him with their hair, whispering
"little one, little one . . ."
and letting down, one by one, their leaves, or flakes of snow,
until his hair is white
and he is crowned with green.

34

The stairs are winding up
beyond the first landing, over
the little nest of rooms
where the fledglings curl warm under
quilts, past the spacious attic room
where dust and the sun dance
in concert every afternoon, the motes
floating down as the stairs climb up
into the well of light, into the twisted branches
of the trees.
         Here, the footing gets
tricky, the spiral tightens but
the breathing is easier; everything
lightens. The cobwebs brush your face,
you break through clouds—the blue
astounds you.
         You are standing
on the second landing, cobalt
laced with light. There are no bearings
you can take; it is too bright
for stars, and the sun turns away
even a sidelong glance. You only know
how high you are from the birds
circling below like particles of dust
whirled in the light.
         The change
is imperceptible at first—the slightest shift
of air, the stairs grow strange
under your feet, the railing
slowly roughens like a branch
of coral lightly furred with green, soft
as the hair of the newly born, sweet
to the fingertips. The blue deepens
as you climb toward night, thickens
till it is too dense to tell
from sea; you pass like a needle
through deep velvet, threading your way
up until you reach
              acorns of light
hung among the highest branches,
swaying easy in the wind.

                    Your hand
still reaching up, encounters nothing;
the elements themselves support you—
a boat scrapes on the beach. You make
the landing. The earth
you climbed so far to reach
is under your feet.

36

—for Fontaine

The home she made was almost sky,
a something evanescent and assured,
a filmy globe so light
it shifted with the slightest breeze.

It was a kind of promise with its skin
stretched tight, so thin
it would have been transparent but
when she breathed, the walls would cloud

and vision soften. At times, when she was tired
there was a tinkling sound
like something delicately breaking
or wind chimes in a garden miles away.

At night, when the gate scraped on its hinges,
she'd dream a woman, statuesque,
a gown that hung in folds creased even
as a column, her eyes light blue

and blank. It was those eyes without the shadow
of a pupil, a pale blue so fierce
that it seemed white, that might have
warned her. Or the hairline cracks

across the blue, a crackle glaze
that it took centuries
to fire, its beauty in
its strange response to heat.

That was years ago. You wouldn't recognize
her house today, the way the cracks have
widened and the wind pours in
like water. Birds float across the blue
gap where the roof is broken, like leaves
across the surface of a pond in late September.

The earth is harrowed in the yard
against the season; the plants turned under
at the end of summer. You can see her chair at twilight
tipped back against the vines
woven on the rough frame of the doorway.

37

And the light that falls
through the partly opened door
is slanting on the yard, a wedge of yellow
in the darkness of the ground. Unless,
as the growing stalk splits
the avocado seed, the ground is
cloven by
the rising of the light.

38

"... the great globe itself,
Yea, all which it inherit, shall dissolve ..."

Extraordinary. Our friends,
the skeptics, who are
ourselves, such an extravagance
of feints, the perfectly spun
glass, exquisite complications, saying
they know that they know nothing,
the oldest ruse. Let it go.
Say what you know.

For once, be rid of the urn
with beauty chased in half-relief, the urn
with the false bottom, the ancient goad
to thirst—the right word turned
exactly on itself. Say what you know.

The glass is raised,
the perfect globe in which
the saint's heart sat, preserved.
The edges of the relic curl
like the tips of starfish drying
or paper that the fire catches.
The air pours in, until it seems
that the invisible has won. A fact,
it is invaded. A moment, it is dust.
Undone—this dust
you leave to air, where
it will dance and light
will catch it in the ordinary way—

it will seem then, as it does now, as if
a burden had been lifted.
The way your hair spreads out around you
in the stream, when the stream
takes it, the way things
lose their weight
when they rest upon the waters.

39

iv. Attrition

"Whose woods these are I think I know."

The landings had gone wrong; white silk,
like shrouds, covered the woods.
The trees had trapped the flimsy fabric
in their web—everywhere the harnessed bodies
hung—helpless, treading air
like water.
        We thought to float down
easily—a simple thing
like coming home: feet first,
a welcome from the waiting fields,
a gentle fall in clover.

We hadn't counted on this
wilderness, the gusts of wind
that took us over; we were surprised
by the tenacity of branching wood,
its reach, and how impenetrable
the place we left, and thought we knew,
could be.
        Sometimes now, as we sway, unwilling
pendulums that mark the time,
we still can dream
someone will come and cut us down.
There is nothing here but words, the calls
we try the dark with—hoping for a human
ear, response, a rescue party.
But all we hear is other
voices like our own, other bodies
tangled in the lines,
the repetition of a cry from every tree:

I can't help you, help me.

43

It was a long fall, that particular
year—the leaves stayed full on the branch
a long time, as if they would be green
forever. Then they reddened slowly as
a blush on the cheeks of someone
slow to anger. When the winds came,
finally, with the icy snarl of winter,
the leaves all seemed to fall at once—
like the armies of a more romantic age,
line on line of uniform red, falling
on the first command to fire.

The woods filled up with red, and the lawns;
the snow came the same night
and covered them; all winter, change
was only the slow shifting
of the drifts, the deepening
and the attrition. When the spring thaw
came at last, the leaves
were too wet to scatter, were something between
what they had been and earth.

When we stumbled on the first
of the bodies in the woods, we found
the snow had kept it perfect. That lifelike
look, that posture of some endless patience
with the way things are; the eyes wide,
the lashes crusted over with white crystals.
Until the sun came out.
                              Now the spring air smells
in that lingering way of a house when
something's crawled into the walls and died there.
But there won't be any finding, no—
only something, once alive, is in there, slowly,
outside of our reach, unwinding.

44

The gaze directed down
into the pool's
green eye. There, it blinks again.
If you are quiet, wait, and do not move,
the shifting green begins
to soften, blur—and then,
within this gentler vision,
the cheat is clear.
               Flies are
everywhere, the gray gauze
of their wings a frenzied
scrim over the water, excited
by the smell of things
fermenting, they skim
the surface scum of algae
on the water, impasto that prevents
reflection.
            It is as if
the world were a dispute, a foolish
dialectic, in which
the middle term is always missing, unless
you count the lily on its pad,
a fallen white wax star, suspended
in the center of the pond.
                  While in the dark
below its flat green raft, the roots
dangle, moving
as the water moves,
           a hopeless, squirming
      snarl.

45

All morning
I have been reading poems
from Vietnam by veterans (the Latin, *veteranus*,
old) young men
stunned into a deadpan
diction, writing between clenched
teeth, the way words bypass tears, step over
bodies on the road gone down too far
for any turning back.
                    Step over,
we are standing at the edge:
"if you have a home in hell
and a farm in Vietnam, sell it
and go home."

The green bags are tagged and shipped;
the faithful Buddhist hearts are quiet
in their jars. The water buffalo
is standing, as he always stood, in the field
that will no longer fill a bowl of rice.
Why does he turn from us, so leisurely, as if
no one were here? And walk away
with plodding steps, unhurried—
his swaying haunches
growing larger with the distance,
his hoofs ringing like temple bells
on the once green earth
of Vietnam.

46

A few flakes of snow, hesitant, fell first;
damp branches, for a time, extinguished them.
But soon they were growing
thick as wool on a winter flank.
The howl of a wolf, slinking off through the snow,
protested its whitening fur, aged in an hour.
The great eyes of the owl filled up with snow.
The lighted squares of window swirled, went out.
The sky descended to the earth
with a cold condescension; the drifts made
artificial hills, the shape of the land shifted,
the signs blurred, the road
vanished. The scaled cones, like fish
carved out of wood, hung ornamental
in the whitened waves of fir. The silence
thickened. A herd of running deer
went up in silver smoke.

The eagle
down from the eyrie to hunt, circles
the white expanse and soars
homeward, talons clamped
on the squirming air
a last flurry of light
snow.

We are the fugitives: buzzards circle us
long before we die. Fire speaks to us
in tongues
we can't decipher, can't resist.
And the cheetah tracks us
through the wood; as the vines brush by,
electric on the wrist, we fear
entanglement, but dread
exposure in the open places more.
We move, and move again, but cannot leave
the valley of the cheetah—we know
the mountain pass is narrow, and sense
the cats above us, crouching;
can almost feel their weight
like boulders on our backs.

So we are patterned by pursuit: part grass
in silence, leave no wake; ford streams
to drown our scent and double back;
keep sentries standing while we sleep.
And still our sleep is light and fitful.

We have no meeting halls, no temple domes
to guard us from the sky.
We value only what we carry on our backs,
portable altars. For these the artists carve
small idols—muscular and smooth,
their gold coats painted on, black
smudges for the spots, and for the eyes
(they spend hours on the eyes)
green jewels incised
with the crisscross markings of our flight,
fugitive trails cut across
the green valley of the cheetah, cracks
in the eyes of the cat.

The saws are coming now, we hear
their high-pitched whine, we see
their silver teeth whirl on the wheel
like Eastern prayers
to gods grown thick with arms.

A man comes slowly from the crowd
and speaks, with that light burr of those
who live with kin where much is
shared and little
needs to be explained. Such living
softens speech, and sharpens

blades. You'd need the cunning
of the innocent in times like these
to catch *those* ears.

If I had been more eloquent
perhaps . . .
we could have lived, the two of us,
the tree out there to bear us
witness. But you could not have come away with me,
and they, of course they wouldn't listen.

Listen, you can hear the silver
buzz saw in the air.
                    To whom am I speaking now?
That *you* is curled up in the inner ear,
a tiny fetus of the crowd that one day might return
singing: holy holy holy.
                    Unless it is a fossil
rolled in there, perfect and resonant,
so what seems life, the stirring of the just
beginning, isn't—
is like a tuning fork that's struck: it seems
to sing, but *isn't   isn't   isn't.*

49

". . . his speeches, his receptions, the *marches
de soutien*, the new appointments: court news.
Actual events are small."

Like this, too, at home. Court speeches,
the gilt-edged glass of pageantry, the pomp
of alliances, desperate matings
done up in braided gold. The swan of ice;
the crystal chandelier
shivers in the fevered light.
The dancers' skins are spotted
with its shattered white—like deer,
flushed from the thickets
of gladiolas arranged along the wall,
bristling like bayonets.
                 The women step
across the floor, something between
a march and minuet, stately,
keeping time, their necks swaying
like stems.
          The tide is coming in the door;
the wet foam swirls across the marble
floor, curling the edges of
their flimsy silver slippers. The air
is heavy as damask, glittering
with salt.
          Below the stairs,
the ancient women climb
into bed alone, each night
more painfully; the old support of bone
turning to menace at the end.

v. Illuminated Manuscripts

Here in our room
the light slips through the fingers,
the window slits cut high in the stone
walls; there is no sound
but the small scratching
of the pens, the noiseless slide of the brush
across white parchment.

Here we work unceasing for the others
while they labor; we're here to—well, to
save them, so we're told: us, with our
itching habits, our little pots
of gilt and ultramarine—the blue
we've pressed from berries.
We are the scribes of the unacknowledged world,
illuminators of the book we torture
with profusion: with foliage, flowers, beasts and
saints in strange positions.

We seldom speak.
The windows are too high, and
then again too slender
for anything but sky. If we look up we see
only a rule of brilliant blue, and that's
the light we work by. We are the brothers
who confess each other, and so
we ought to know how little
humility is ours. We dream our patience
will reward us; we take our time.

Yesterday I went out to our garden
and saw up on the hill
a cross a peasant planted—was it
just last winter? —a simple cross
of wood he'd bound together with a piece of twine
to mark the place the earth had taken
what he had thought was his. It looked to me,
who spends my days illuminating letters,
like a T. But it was almost lost in foliage, a vine
had caught it with a tendril and obscured it
with the leaves; it was perplexed by
wildflowers, and nearly gone in green.

That's why I went tonight to see
that farmer—knocked on his door and said to him:
forgive me. He stared at me in dumb dismay
and shook because I seemed a holy man, and mad, to him—
a little man in a frayed robe, gold-spattered,
with paint stains on his fingers, apologizing
for what he couldn't know
had never mattered.

54

Mist, the weather changing.
And clouds close in, covering the break
of day. The light will come with rain.

Men, small and ragged as torn flags,
flutter in the gray. The distant lines
of mountains are as indistinct
as eyebrows on the faces of the old.
The whispering dragon
of the brush . . . the mist it breathes
out on the page . . . the waves
that open till they're oceans.
Your eyes forget
the solid world: the bruises
of the rocks, the black strokes
of bamboo, your anxious cry
lost in the tumult of the waterfall.
The rain has begun in the mountains.

The distant water has no waves
but reaches up and touches
cloud. The vanishing point is
everywhere the brush moves
heavy with water, waving away
the object world, going gray
into the gray water—and we
are the little men running, running
from the dawn, the dawn that is coming after us,
the rising wave we can't outrun,
but can turn, at the last moment, to record
its magnificent lift, the tons of water
poised over us—as if
too beautiful to break.

55

It was something flawless,
something about the mountain: perhaps it was
the way the cherry trees
in their spring whitening, echoed the snow
in its composure at the top. So to
confound the butterfly
with the drifting of a petal to the branch
was to make the perfect
error. Or to arrange a piece of earth, a stone
and stunted tree, was to have the planet
in a bowl. Or breaking waves arrested
at their peak, arabesques
of the cut wood, the perfectly inked
block. So when the sword is drawn
and lifted high above the head,
its vertical divides
the mountain neatly into halves.
When the sword falls, the mountain is whole
again, past understanding,
standing over
the sundered body at its feet.

56

There might be woods out there; it's much
too dark to tell. We talk
of what we think we know, to make the dark
resemblance. Out there, we hear a crashing
in the brush, the sound a body makes
when nature bends to it, for a moment,
in passing. We keep embellishing
the edges of that sound
with our own bright tales.

A burning twig snaps in the fire.
Our muscles tense, ears strain; alert,
the body answers to the world
long before the mind has tracked it.
The crashing in the brush seems nearer:
we hear it just beyond the place
the shadows start their transit into black.
We don't dare leave our fire, begin
to chatter like the birds
who take the unexpected in their bills
and worry it to some familiar shape,
as a bear will lick her newborn cub
to life, that body she has worn inside
but doesn't know until her tongue
has torn away its veil.

Just then, the dark divides, as if
a piece of nature had come loose,
detached itself from wood, or countryside.

It is only a man in country clothes, his eyes
red from weeping, or wine, or from the bright
reflection of our fire. He stumbles
among us, sits down. We see the silver
where the fire lights his hair, and try—
with the reflex of our kind—to coax him
into speech. He doesn't answer, doesn't
speak, but looks to us
in mute appeal, implores us
like some ancient mariner who's lost
his story.

He slept, at least we think he slept.
We drank, and sat till late and stared into the fire.
And there was something dark and shapely
outlined by the tongues of flame—as if someone
were walking in the center of the fire,
silent as the shadow of a stone, but
moving, unconsoled, just like a man.

58

Out there,
the scene that won't compare
with one we thought to stumble on
unbidden, the hidden clearing
in a wood that deep
inside a book one day in childhood
we had been promised as
a secret garden: there, where
the invalid boy you weren't supposed
to cherish, got up and walked, and
words hung dark and ripe
as berries in their clusters
you only thought were shadows,
sweet to the tongue and
guarded by the spiders, spinning webs
without a thought
to their design; it was just
that silk came easy from their flesh,
outlined their swinging in the air
with silver. As our mothers
the makers of lace, their fingers
all eyes, their eyes clouding over
with years—in time
had lost all sight of their design
as they grew better
at its manufacture.

We could wish ourselves their fate
and not avert it—the subtlety
of snowflakes on the tongue
gone in the instant of their falling.
We could wish for
such perfection, such dissolving . . .

59

When looking in a pool on a quiet day—
the water shows your face to you, but
this is no mythical event. You are no
Narcissus, rooted to the spot, passion
turning to purple petals by the pond.
Reflections are a trick of light,
the same effect is possible
in the cheapest bathroom mirror.
However, with pools, when you toss a pebble
at your face, it will dissolve
like an old pudding; the light, after all,
requiring a placid surface
for untroubled imitation. This proves
not only that myths are old hat, but that
mimetic art is dead, we are all
a stone's throw from dissolution, and
other modern notions. Two things, however,
require comment: 1) three minutes after
your face shatters, and the ripples
in proverbial fashion, spread to the edges
of the known world—you will return, as whole
as ever, nearly symmetrical, if not
unshakable: a return to contend with.
2) When the bear bends over the pool
to drink, he sees a pair of huge
gossamer wings beating over his shoulders
and a pair of slender pink arms
where his paws ought to be. This proves
that mimetic art is not dead, that bears,
when they are drinking, are poetically
inclined, and that the muses
still perform, damp with inspiration
at the occasional watering spot.

60

One day we round the last blind
corner of the town; enter the square
to find the old palazzo masked,
its towers gray above
the scaffolding of restoration,
great sheets of straw hung over walls;
behind, perhaps, men slowly crawl
rebuilding the facade, painting in
the faded forms; at least,
we think they must be working there
restoring what they think it is they saw.
Outside all supposition is the straw,
the scaffolding is all we have to go on.

As the subway diggers
in Fellini's Rome, the last Rome of the dream,
could not be sure the fresco that they saw
was ever there, so close it matched the frightened flight
of image in the mind, so soon it crumbled at the touch
of air, and spectres fled
like dust motes in erratic beams
of flashlights in a hundred trembling hands,
and vanished in the glare
of daylight as they broke the tunnel through.

Like sentient outlaws, we can't sleep—
but wake from one dream to another.
Each rise we top reveals the same
enormous boulders of the same dry riverbed,
the backbone of a prehistoric force, stranded
by the water when it fled. And the sea
keeps retreating as we near,
the tide keeps going out, as if the moon
were always racing toward China:
the long march of the waves, growing as they go,
until the ocean seems some phototropic beast
forever bent on light.

The fern is weaving
its fronds through the shaded air—too
delicate to mix with sun, a fragile
nearly nonexistent green, a tracery
so fine it seems aesthetic, a recluse
in a public world of pines.

                              A breeze so light
and insubstantial, it doesn't move
the leaves, will bring a shower of spores
to earth, the way dust drifts down
in a spoke of light, the way
dry needles and the moss
must turn the fall of foot to muted sound,
all movement to a hush, a passing rustle
in the dusk that lasts.

The fern can seem an eden to the ant,
who likes to sit beside it and forget
the black collective hum of hill,
the shrill that keeps it dragging
bits of stuff—ant following ant—into
that gaping place in ground where
all lines end and vanish with their purpose.

As if these lines that lace
the earth with trails we read in
lieu of some design, did not compel us
in their trace, our jaws set tight around
whatever we have salvaged from above
to fill the dark and vaulted space.
Below, the slow enormous building
of some great cathedral made of wisps
goes on—the bits of straw, of leaf,
the dried husks of the pods—
are handed down like judgments
from the opening in the hill
to build those withered spires reaching
down, a sanctuary—upside down—furnished
like a pharoah's tomb with all the stale
regalia of another world that won't
suffice; those spires thrusting
toward the center of the earth, a homing
we begin to question

62

as some heroic chore whose real completion
will leave us where we were before.

I want to go back faithful
to the fern—to feel again
the faded air, light shudder, the fall
of weightless spores, the slight
green tremor on the forest floor.

63

After all
these years of hating
the first-person singular, the one rent
in the good fabric: the lost solar voice
that spoke like lightning on a summer night
when the air lowered over earth,
almost the heavy breath of God—refusing
to break into any kind of rain, that thick air
where every drop of sweat was one more
rise in the humidity, every wish another
frozen flash of light; and the flowers slowly
dried, their petals, singed
by the sun's forbidding
light, fell, one by one, onto the paths
where people walked alone or in
oppressive clusters, always hoping
for the hunter's gun to break
the thick bushes into birds—loving the sight
of scattered flight, birds tossed
out on the sky like rice
at a wedding no one wanted.

Now it is good to watch
the birds gathered on the ground
where the seed has spilled on the snow.
We feed them all in that companionable way
Greeks leave fresh water in the bottles placed
in little altars by the fields. We've left
the wide waters where the old ships
used to plow their furrows, lines
of worry to disturb
the serene brow of the sea.
The taste of salt from our own bright veins
closes the wound; we turn away
from tracing those unimportant scars,
those roads we used to walk like pilgrims
on the trail of an old injury:
mea culpa mea culpa   why me?   ringing
their dry antiphonies in the brain.

We leave our kites caught in the trees—
these scraps of an ancient entertainment,
an old foolishness about flight,
with strings attached—we leave them
to the mercies of
the rough branch, the tearing wind, the last
dissolve of rain.
And when jets streak the sky
with their melting trails of smoke,
we are glad to be down here,
safe from the silver bellies
of the air's metallic whales: down here
where the furrows in the garden will fuzz over soon
with green, vanish into the lush cover
we coax from what
we can no longer see: the lines
that grow green again, then
wonderfully, most wonderfully, are gone. . . .

65

The misted sun we used to love
has washed up brilliant on this distant shore
just as we dreamed it.
                        Here, the zones
are sharp—the day a dazzled white,
the night a perfect blank, without
transition. The daily blaze of light
is followed by the hurtling fall of dark
without the slow-blue-going of the northern dusk,
without the softening dawn, the ground-mist
that obscures the world while something shapes
itself inside, secure against intrusion.
But here the morning found us
of a sudden, half-made from one shape
to another, the scrawls
of some unfinished drawing, crawling on the beach,
startled, uncompleted, by the light.

We watch
with eyes jarred open, the slow foam breaking
on the circle we must wake in, we
who wanted knowledge of
what we'd become by leaving
the cloudy solace of our home.
For this the compass was invented, the stars
were charted like a trail—crumbs
of light—to follow to this island.

We have begun to grow a longing, the fur
of animals transplanted to the tropics,
but still expecting winter. And sometimes
in the night it almost seems
the island has begun to move, and caught
the current, till it will come
upon a continent in shadow
and add itself to old convulsions of the coast
—peninsula—
an oar the land dipped in
at the last moment
to keep itself from sliding out to sea.

I. Evening Flight

(for Bob)

Shh, the light is whispering, soft, day's end.

And darkness comes again, another way: late, lingering
and long, leaves warmth as it replaces light—
as tenderness comes after
anger, turning away, a hand
touches your arm, twilight

a bright smear across a fading sky.

The wind is hushed; the birds becalmed out on the bay
begin to stir, first with a shudder
of feathers, then
a white churn of water
at their feet, then the steep climb
to where the sun just was—
a lantern disappearing into brush.

Fireflies . . .
the sparks where dusk
is welded to the night; the wind
begins again, and dark eyes
open in the wood. You can hear
the trees breathing,

the flying squirrel stretched

ᶜor a moment in the space between
two branches and the owl:
a warm furred x floating in the sky
on wings of flesh, it skims the wide
and dizzy height, fearless as those

themselves unknown, who know the branch
is waiting on the other side.

II. Lifeline

(for Sonia Sanchez)

The old bridges are down
that led this way, blown up.
We've had to improvise with bits
of rope, knots
from a thousand ends: a macramé of old,
entropic bonds—bell ropes, the bucket ropes
from wells long since gone dry,
the ropes the Brothers of Saint Francis wore
about their rough brown habits, as a sign.

Space stares at us above and from below; our loss
has built this swaying bridge across
the vacancy. Everything makes it
sway: wind, your weight, a passing flock
of birds, the earth's turning, even the whispering
dead that seem to issue from below
like steam from fissures in the distant
ground. Sometimes it seems a web, miraculous,
thrown by some solar spider in the blinding light
of noon: a promise to step out on, or a trap.
Though we remember knotting it, it seems
impossible, the work of other hands, or forces
whose weaving we comprise, but cannot map—
though we must now trust all our weight
to its design: a little band
with quaking legs, afraid to look
to either left or right, hand over hand across
this breathless space, the way that climbers
pick their way up rock, afraid to move until a hand
has found its purchase on the slope.
But we're not climbing any more, just inching
slow across this fragile, swaying line—
praying that the knots will hold.

Out here, the wind is strong, tossed
on a blanket of air, we're dizzy from
the wild arcs we're trying to cross on.
We cling like insects to a blade of grass, depending
on a line of green that bends
and will spring back the second
that they leave it. No going back.

68

Hand over hand,

        slow, don't look down.

Hand over hand,

        steady, keep your head

where your feet,

        must go: step,

           don't breathe

step

The space is wide. It might take days, or years,
to cross. This time, to put our fear inside
parentheses, we're forced to think
of what we'll find there on the other side.

Ah, so you thought we had a master
plan, had built this bridge with something large
in mind, some sure ambition waiting, Jerusalem—
beyond this great divide. No doubt you'd heard
of how the Spanish left a green land fat with sheep
for gold. How their mind's eye crossed the sea,
saw burnished towers, set sail with an impatience
only the wind could fill, the ocean quench. The sun
set at perpetual noon. Well, we are a kind of sunburned
Spain, disabused of gold, wearing
the bright blankets of the Indians
who died in our tracks.

We go the way of birds
who migrate by the sound of tides
pulling at the continents as they fly,
who keep returning to a nesting place
where the grass is long, the cover good,
the broken shells attest
the long success of generation.
Some will leave their eggs there, others—bones.
If we can pass this space, this wilderness we cleared
in our first crossing. Now, in the last cat's cradle
we could string, we're trying to go home.
But the wind decides.

Meanwhile, swaying in the gray
air, we pick our way
and dream the earth
we left behind
is waiting on the other side.

70

THE
JUNIPER
PRIZE

This volume is the fifth recipient
of the Juniper Prize,
presented annually by the
University of Massachusetts Press
for a volume of original poetry.
The prize is named in honor of Robert Francis,
who has lived for many years at
Fort Juniper, Amherst, Massachusetts.

Library of Congress Cataloging in Publication Data
Wilner, Eleanor.
Maya.
I. Title.
PS3573.I45673M3   811'.5'4   79-4753
ISBN 0-87023-277-0
ISBN 0-87023-278-9 pbk.